C000063208

Vintage Stitching

Treasury

**MORE THAN 400 AUTHENTIC
EMBROIDERY DESIGNS**

Suzanne McNeill

DESIGN ORIGINALS

an Imprint of Fox Chapel Publishing
www.d-originals.com

Contents

ISBN 978-1-4972-0007-4

COPY PERMISSION: The written instructions, photographs, designs, patterns, and projects in this publication are intended for the personal use of the reader and may be reproduced for that purpose only. Any other use, especially commercial use, is forbidden under law without the written permission of the copyright holder. Every effort has been made to ensure that all information in this book is accurate. However, due to differing conditions, tools, and individual skills, neither the author nor publisher can be responsible for any injuries, losses, or other damages which may result from the use of the information in this book.

INFORMATION: All rights reserved. All images in this book have been reproduced with the knowledge and prior consent of the artists concerned and no responsibility is accepted by producer, publisher, or printer for any infringement of copyright or otherwise, arising from the contents of this publication. Every effort has been made to ensure that credits accurately comply with information supplied.

WARNING: Due to the components used in this craft, children under 8 years of age should not have access to materials or supplies without adult supervision. Under rare circumstances components of products could cause serious or fatal injury. Please read all safety warnings for the products being used. Neither New Design Originals, the product manufacturer, or the supplier is responsible.

NOTE: The use of products and trademark names is for informational purposes only, with no intention of infringement upon those trademarks.

© 2015 by Suzanne McNeill and New Design Originals Corporation, www.d-originals.com, an imprint of Fox Chapel Publishing, 800-457-9112, 1970 Broad Street, East Petersburg, PA 17520.

This book contains selected content from Vintage Animals (978-1-57421-587-8), Vintage Tinted Linens and Quilts (978-1-57421-462-8), Vintage Garden Quilts (978-1-57421-561-8), Vintage Home Linens and Quilts (978-1-57421-512-0), Ladies of Leisure (978-1-57421-516-8), Linen Heirlooms: Vintage Linens (978-1-57421-785-8), Tied Up! (978-1-57421-468-0) and Redwork in Blue (978-1-57421-749-0).

Hand stitching for the projects featured on front cover done by Anna Mae Roth, Milford, Nebraska. Thanks, Mom! —Carole

Printed in Singapore
First printing

Introduction

For nearly a century, the wonderful relaxing pastime of art embroidery entertained women through the U.S. and much of the world. No one thought much of it while they were doing it; after all, it was just something to pass the time, making a thoughtful gift for a friend or a treat for oneself. So little consideration has been given to this facet of textile history that some experts cringe when they hear "art embroidery" applied to the stamped goods and transfers our mothers and grandmothers bought for a dollar (or a penny!) from the variety store. But art embroidery is indeed what the magazines and pattern publishers and catalogs called those fanciful designs.

As textile historians tend to focus on rarer things, the records and memories of this widely popular form of needlework have been slowly declining. What a rich legacy of ordinary pleasure and simple lives is left unwritten in the fascinating history of art embroidery! Those of you who cherish bluebird-covered dresser scarves and scotties-chasing-kitties tea towels know how compelling the untold story of the woman who made them is. Imagine her story multiplied by millions—that is the scope of art embroidery.

Vintage embroidery lets us reach back and touch an ordinary moment in the past. It records as much as a vintage magazine. The designs provide a record of attitudes, humor, and culture, much of it from a woman's point of view. Everyone who is lucky enough to have a small collection of old linens embroidered by mothers or grandmothers feels the hand reaching across the years. Decorative embroidery was (and is) used on so many household items: linens, pillows, doilies, potholders, kitchen towels, button bags, silverware holders, etc.—you name it and it was probably decorated at some time or other with a bit of embroidery and possibly a touch of tinting.

Now it's your turn to give the designs of the old days new life. This book presents an exciting array of vintage patterns for you to peruse, use, and enjoy. Fantastic flowers and irresistible animals share pages with days-of-the-week motifs and beautiful ladies. The styles are unique to their eras and therefore fascinating looks at the past, with designs in this book dating as far back as the late 1800s, up through the Great Depression, and into the fairytale 1950s. They are nostalgic treasures you can bring alive again. It's time to stitch up the past!

◇◇◇◇◇◇◇◇◇◇◇◇◇◇

Thank you to Nori Koenig for her extensive help, research, and knowledge of vintage linens.

◇◇◇◇◇◇◇◇◇◇◇◇◇◇

Embroidery Styles Through the Years

Here's a tip-of-the iceberg, seat-of-your-pants synopsis of the basic trends of
art embroidery patterns, almost 100 years in less than 500 words!

1880–1900

Realistic or naturalistic renderings. Visual puns and symbolic messages common. "Talking" linens with greetings or jokes. Novelty work done in strong, natural colors. Fine embroidery used for better quality decorative purposes—eyeletting, padded satin stitch, etc. Turkey work/redwork a popular trend, where patterns for Kensington stitch (needlepainting) are done in outlining only, in Turkey Red. First iron-on transfers appear on the market. Bonanza of easily available flosses, fabrics, and patterns suddenly becomes available.

1900–1910

Arts & Crafts style patterns are a special niche in the kit and pattern market. Simplified natural forms (flowers and abstract forms) often combine some very curvilinear elements of art nouveau. Many kits pre-tinted to show elaborate stitching plans. This tinting is often simply outlined and left to be enjoyed on its own.

1900–1920

Novelty patterns become increasingly professional looking. Novelty motifs continue to be increasingly realistic. Fine embroidery motifs continue in eyeletting and other traditional methods.

1920s

Kits for embroidered everything, from clothes to umbrella holders, are available. Incredible number of patterns published. It's a golden era for art embroidery. Linens feature unusually shaped edges and corners, often fitting tightly to motifs. Colonial Lady themes begin popularity. There is increasing whimsy and stylization in many designs. Black highlights and accents are common in light pastel color schemes. Tinting becomes increasingly common in combination with embroidery.

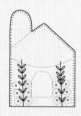

1930s

Patterns are highly professional, standardized. Motifs tend toward lush shapes, colors, or backgrounds. Boudoir pillows, potholders, and Day of the Week towels become increasingly popular. Novelty dolls, pajama bags, and other objects combine tinting, sewing, and embroidery. Styles are influenced by Art Deco—strong shapes and luxurious colors. Black is used as a background color for a stark, rich effect.

1940s

War-conscious patterns appear, including stuffed soldier dolls and motifs of soldiers with girls, etc. Patterns take on slightly cartooned features, such as chipmunk cheeks and especially large eyes, on a consistent basis, similar to other cartoon artwork of the period. Variety of shapes in linens decreases, leading to less complex hems and finishing. Period details are commonly used to add life to patterns. Increasingly refined patterns mimic the real world, but always as a caricature.

1950s

Patterns move from being highly rendered to being occasionally over-rendered (action lines, etc.) and complicated. Period details are no longer found. There are fewer pattern publishers to choose from. Elaborately feminine designs feature figures and lines consistent with the elegant fashions of the times.

Color Gallery

In this gallery you will find a selection of both vintage and contemporary items, all stitched using vintage patterns. The patterns are used on an incredibly wide variety of items, from table runners and quilts to handkerchiefs and laundry bags. Use this gallery as inspiration for your own lovely homemade stitchings.

The fascination with humanizing pets became popular in the 1920s. Puppies, kittens, and other species enjoyed their leisure time in very human ways. Active animals were not limited to kids' items, but showed up throughout the house, especially in the kitchen. (Patterns on pages 73, 74, 100, and 131.)

Unmistakably art deco, the top pillow updated 1930s Colonial style with background tinting. The fruit basket tablecloth corner in the middle shows how pattern companies would often update popular patterns to keep them fresh, leading to somewhat eclectic results. The bluebird pattern at the bottom dates back to the 1940s, though its style and subject reach back to the turn of the century. (Patterns on pages 144, 56, and 63.)

The rectangular pillow shown here combines the silhouette trend of the 1920s and 1930s with the pastel palette of boudoir pillows. The colors of the square pillow make a big impact when contained within the black outlining that was classic in the 1920s. (Patterns on pages 116 and 156.)

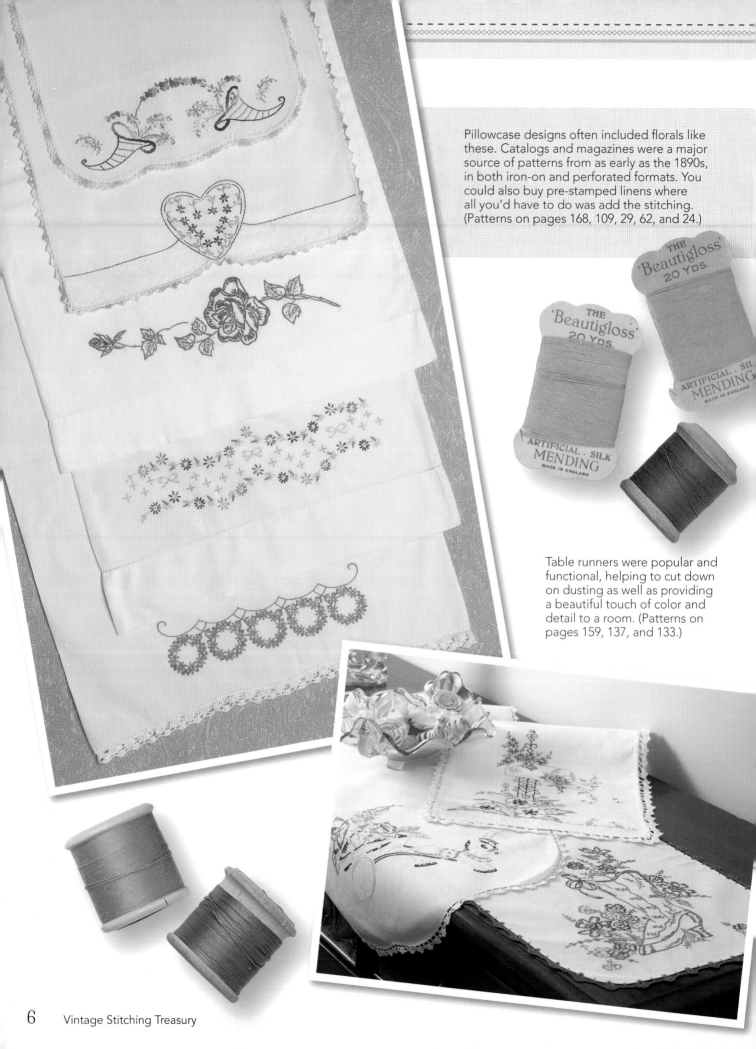

Pillowcase designs often included florals like these. Catalogs and magazines were a major source of patterns from as early as the 1890s, in both iron-on and perforated formats. You could also buy pre-stamped linens where all you'd have to do was add the stitching. (Patterns on pages 168, 109, 29, 62, and 24.)

Table runners were popular and functional, helping to cut down on dusting as well as providing a beautiful touch of color and detail to a room. (Patterns on pages 159, 137, and 133.)

Bonnet babes like the pink and blue lady were a perpetual favorite on all types of linens, including laundry bags. Girls fighting to hang their wash in the wind were a popular motif in the 1930s and 1940s. Graceful lines and lithe figures were common for the ladies' shapes. (Patterns on pages 174 and 126.)

Bunnies and balloons were favorite 1940s and 1950s themes. The finishing details and style of the bunny crib sheet suggest it was time-consuming to finish, but think again. Skillful design made the most of limited embroidery, allowing most crib sheets to be easily and quickly made. The doggie trio crib sheet design dates back to the 1930s and tells a little story, like many crib sheets. (Patterns on pages 157 and 186.)

The practice of assigning a task to each day of the week on a towel was immensely popular beginning in the 1920s and still interests many people today. The chores depicted were often the same from series to series, including staples like washing, baking, shopping, and rest or church on Sunday. (Patterns on pages 152–153 and 160–161.)

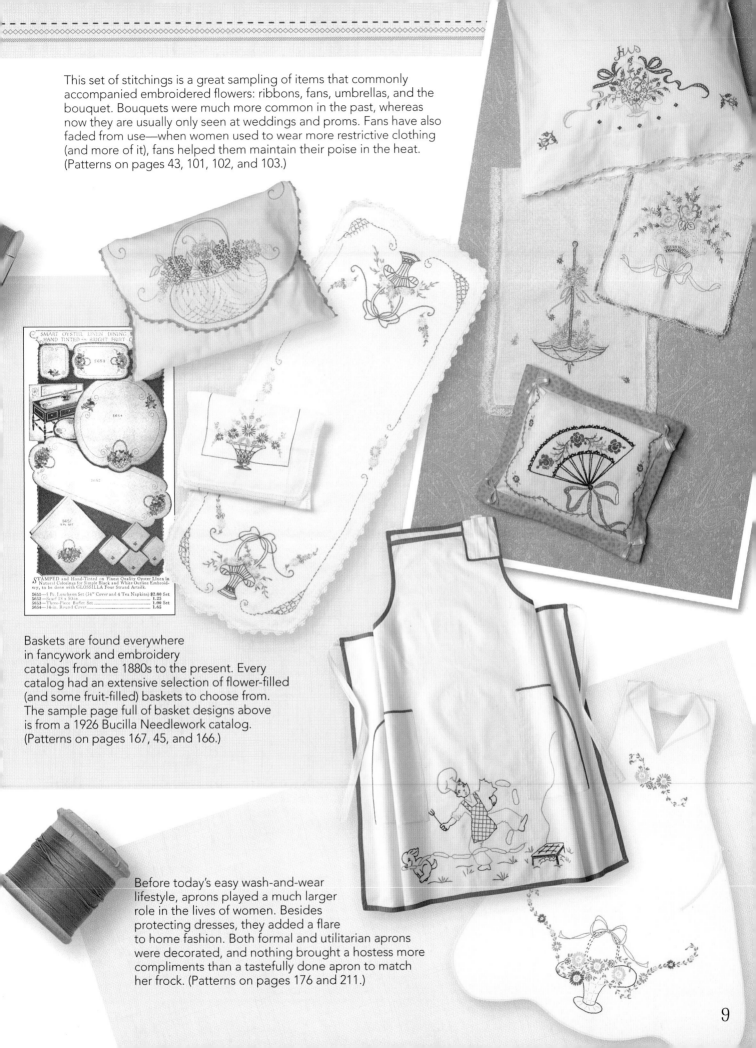

This set of stitchings is a great sampling of items that commonly accompanied embroidered flowers: ribbons, fans, umbrellas, and the bouquet. Bouquets were much more common in the past, whereas now they are usually only seen at weddings and proms. Fans have also faded from use—when women used to wear more restrictive clothing (and more of it), fans helped them maintain their poise in the heat. (Patterns on pages 43, 101, 102, and 103.)

Baskets are found everywhere in fancywork and embroidery catalogs from the 1880s to the present. Every catalog had an extensive selection of flower-filled (and some fruit-filled) baskets to choose from. The sample page full of basket designs above is from a 1926 Bucilla Needlework catalog. (Patterns on pages 167, 45, and 166.)

Before today's easy wash-and-wear lifestyle, aprons played a much larger role in the lives of women. Besides protecting dresses, they added a flare to home fashion. Both formal and utilitarian aprons were decorated, and nothing brought a hostess more compliments than a tastefully done apron to match her frock. (Patterns on pages 176 and 211.)

9

Potholders have been and always will be a necessity in every kitchen, old or new. They can also be a decorative accent. Sets that include both pads and holders are a vintage favorite. They often contained two pads and a sleeve with hooks, and the patterns were usually sold as a kit. (Patterns on pages 220, 173, and 136.)

I rule the Roost

I rule the Rooster

A Man Works from Sun to Sun,

Woman's Work is Never Done.

THE Beautigloss 20 YDS.

ARTIFICIAL . SILK MENDING MADE IN ENGLAND

Embroidery as a decorative art was not only useful, but provided an enjoyable break from heavier household tasks. Vintage designs provide a lovely record of attitudes, humor, and current culture from a woman's point of view. Whimsical, funny, and sometimes tongue-in-cheek vintage designs remain popular today because of their charm. (Patterns on pages 33 and 123.)

These delightful samples show a very popular practice of intricate embroidery designs with crocheted trim. Many patterns from the 1920s through the 1930s called for the addition of crocheted designs to adorn the edges of items, adding a delicate and fancy feel to pieces. (Patterns on pages 71, 178, and 158.)

Baby quilts were and still are a great favorite, adding color and style to a nursery as well as teaching and entertaining the children who own them. Animals were a popular and natural subject for nursery décor. Victorian designs were quite realistic, but by the 1920s animals had become more stylized, and in the 1930s and 1940s, they had become more like characters. (Patterns on pages 110–111.)

Kitchen linens often included maids, hostesses, or chefs. The chef was almost always as chubby as the maid was shapely. The quilt shown here includes a bit of appliqué on the chef himself. It was popular in the 1930s and 1940s to add this kind of detail to embroidery. (Patterns on pages 64–65.)

Samplers are one of the most well-known types of embroidery. Their styles changed a great deal over the centuries, from their origins as ways to remember patterns that couldn't be recorded any other way, to their use by young girls to practice their stitching "penmanship" of alphabets, to their evolvement into more pictorial designs with many types of stitches, as shown here. (Pattern on page 113.)

This is my sampler...

Embroidery Stitches

Working with Floss

Separate embroidery floss. Use 24" (61cm) lengths of floss and a #8 embroidery needle. Use 2 to 3 ply floss to outline large elements of the design and to embroider larger and more stylized patterns. Use 2 ply for the small details on some items.

Backgrounds

When working with light-colored fabrics, do not carry dark flosses across large unworked background areas. Stop and start again to prevent unsightly "ghost strings" from showing through the front. Another option is to back tinted muslin with another layer of muslin before you add embroidery stitches. This will help keep ghost strings from showing.

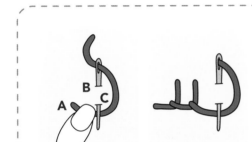

BLANKET STITCH

Come up at A, hold the thread down with your thumb, and go down at B. Come back up at C with the needle tip over the thread. Pull the stitch into place. Repeat, outlining with the bottom legs of the stitch. Use this stitch to edge fabrics.

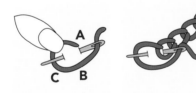

CHAIN STITCH

Come up at A. To form a loop, hold the thread down with your thumb and go down at B (as close as possible to A). Come back up at C with the needle tip over the thread. Repeat to form a chain.

CROSS STITCH

Make a diagonal straight stitch (up at A, down at B) from lower left to upper right. Come up at C and go down at D to make another diagonal straight stitch the same length as the first one. The stitch will form an X.

FRENCH KNOT

Come up at A. Wrap the floss around the needle 2 to 3 times. Insert the needle close to A. Hold the floss and pull the needle through the loops gently.

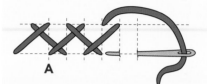

HERRINGBONE STITCH

Come up at A. Make a slanted stitch to the top right, inserting the needle at B. Come up a short distance away at C. Insert the needle at D to complete the stitch. Bring the needle back up at the next A to begin a new stitch. Repeat.

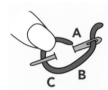

LAZY DAISY STITCH

Come up at A. Go down at B (right next to A) to form a loop. Come back up at C with the needle tip over the thread. Go down at D to make a small anchor stitch over the top of the loop. Come back up at E.

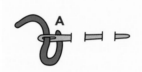

RUNNING STITCH

Come up at A. Weave the needle through the fabric, making short, even stitches. Use this stitch to gather fabrics, too.

SATIN STITCH

Work small straight stitches close together and at the same angle to fill an area with  stitches. Vary the length of the stitches as required to keep the outline of the area smooth.

STRAIGHT STITCH

Come up at A and go down at B to form a simple flat stitch. Use this stitch for hair for animals and for simple petals on small flowers.

STEM STITCH

Work from left to right to make regular, slanting stitches along the stitch line. Bring the needle up above the center of the last stitch. Also called Outline stitch.

WHIP STITCH

Insert the needle under a few fibers of one layer of fabric. Bring the needle up through the other layer of fabric. Use this stitch to attach the folded raw edges of fabric to the back of pieces or to attach bindings around the edges of quilts and coverlets.

Tip: Lightweight iron-on interfacing can be applied to the back of your fabric before you begin your embroidery. This will stabilize the fabric as you stitch. Simply follow the manufacturer's instructions to apply the interfacing. This may eliminate the need for an embroidery frame or hoop. The interfacing is not removed after your stitching is completed.

How to Use the Patterns

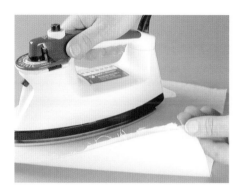

1 **Prepare fabric for patterns.** Prewash the fabric to remove sizing. Mark an X at the center of a piece of freezer paper on the dull side. Place the shiny side of the paper on the wrong side of the quilt block or other fabric piece. Press with an iron for ten seconds. The paper backing protects the pattern you are tracing, especially if you are using ink, and stabilizes the fabric while you trace the design.

2 **Trace designs.** Use the X on the freezer paper as a guide to center the block or fabric piece over the desired pattern to be transferred. Use an .01 pen or a very sharp no. 2 pencil to trace the design onto the right side of the fabric. It may be easier to use a light box or to tape the pattern to a window to trace lines. Remove the freezer paper after transferring the designs.

3 **Embroider designs.** Use 24" (61cm) lengths of floss. Separate the strands of the floss, thread as many strands as you are using into a #8 embroidery needle, and knot one end of floss. Use 2 or 3 ply floss to outline stitch the large elements of the design. Use 1 ply floss for small circles and ovals such as eyes or berries. When you are finished stitching the design, press the completed piece.

Care of Linens

Washing

- Test for colorfastness on the seam allowance. Let several drops of water fall through the fabric onto white blotter paper. If color appears, the fabric is not colorfast.
- To set dye, soak fabric in water and vinegar.
- Wash with a very mild detergent or soap, using tepid water. Follow all label instructions carefully.
- Do not use chlorine bleach on fine linen. Whiten it by hanging it in full sunlight.

Stain Removal

- **Ballpoint ink:** Place on an absorbent material and soak with denatured or rubbing alcohol. Apply room temperature glycerin and flush with water. Finally, apply ammonia and quickly flush with water.
- **Candle wax:** Place fabric between layers of absorbent paper and iron on low setting. Change paper as it absorbs wax. If a stain remains, wash with peroxide bleach.
- **Rust:** Remove with lemon juice, oxalic acid, or hydrofluoric acid.
- **Grease:** Use a presoak fabric treatment and wash in cold water.
- **Nongreasy:** Soak in cold water to neutralize the stain. Apply a presoak and then wash in cold water.

Storage

- Wash and rinse thoroughly in soft water.
- Do not size or starch.
- Place cleaned linen on acid-free tissue paper and roll loosely.
- Line storage boxes with a layer of acid-free tissue paper.
- Place rolled linens in a box. Do not stack. Weight causes creases.
- Do not store linens in plastic bags.
- Hang linen clothing in a muslin bag or cover with a cotton sheet.

Care of Vintage Linens

As vintage linens have become more collectible, many enthusiasts have become textile conservators to their own mini-museums of heirloom dresser scarves, doilies, and days-of-the-week towels. It isn't hard or expensive to store and clean a collection safely, if you take advantage of some common sense—and some new products.

Roll linens to prevent creases

Rolling linens for storage, like Grandma did, was so widely practiced that embroidery kits for decorative linen rolls were popular sellers in turn-of-the-century catalogs! Today, textile experts heartily endorse Grandma's method. Placing a piece of acid-free tissue on the surface of the textile will reduce wrinkles even further. From a practical point of view, rolling may not always be possible. Make sure your most precious linens get this treatment. If you must fold, use acid-free tissue and fold the piece in thirds, not halves. At least then creases won't run right through the middle of the piece.

Acid-free cardboard comes to the rescue

Conservators highly recommend the use of acid-free cardboard boxes to store almost everything— including linens. Why? Air circulation is important to prevent moisture damage—a common culprit when storing textiles. See-through plastic containers, though, are convenient, affordable, and available. If you are going to store in plastic, keep the containers away from the damp, open them regularly, and line them with acid-free tissue. Indulge in the pleasure of examining your collection often, but wear white cotton gloves to keep from adding moisture from your hands.

Think before you wash

Conservators view washing as a last resort for restoring the look of linens. Simply airing textiles to remove musty smells is far safer than washing will ever be—and it's definitely the first step to try. Several products, available at some antique stores, are specially designed for removing yellowing and light stains from linens. Never use an untried product on a treasured heirloom! Try the product out on a few "disposable" vintage scraps to test its stain removal abilities and damage potential.

Modern science vs. the kitchen cupboard

Many antique dealers and quilt shops carry stain removers formulated especially to remove age spots from antique linens. Homemade formulas abound as well. A solution of equal parts of Biz and Cascade has many loyal users, as does baking soda and lemon juice. Remember that washing is only half the battle—rinsing is equally important, because detergent residue actually attracts dirt and oil to fibers. After rinsing, smooth the article carefully on a towel and roll gently to press out moisture. Never, ever wring an heirloom textile item! Lay the piece flat to dry, unless you really don't care if the item is permanently stretched out of shape.

Harness the sun for good—not evil

Mildew stains can be bleached somewhat from white linens by washing them and drying them flat in sunshine. But beware! Direct sunlight is guaranteed to fade any colored textile or embroidery. If your heart is set on cafe curtains from old printed tablecloths, resign yourself to seeing their bright colors fade over time. Glass and sunlight are another combination that textile guardians caution against. A good framer knows to recommend plexiglass or a glass that screens ultraviolet rays when framing your heirloom embroidery.

Tinting with Crayons

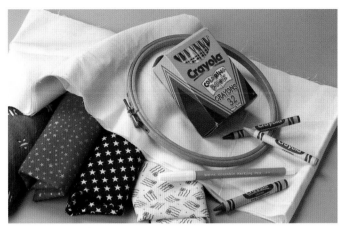

Only a few basic supplies are needed.

Besides being convenient and inexpensive, crayons come in beautiful colors. Simply color in the spaces to create the look you want. But tinting with crayons definitely requires a unique technique. Even though ironing softens crayons, their hard nature means that some of the texture of the fabric and the strokes you make will show through—just like when you make a rubbing over a penny. Practice your crayon tinting technique on scrap pieces of muslin first.

Tip: Let the fabric do the work. A printed fabric (white on white or off-white) adds depth to your shading.

Supplies
You'll need muslin fabric, crayon colors, embroidery floss, embroidery hoop, blue-line water erase pen, and a needle.

Build Up Color, Edges In

Different strokes will change the way the piece looks.

Add layers of crayon color with the strokes going in one direction, or opposite directions for a darker effect. Start lightly—you can always add more. Shading built up from the edges inward helps model or add depth to pieces, so that the tinted areas are not only colorful but three-dimensional as well.

Use the Correct End
For filling in color, the blunt end of the crayon works best.

1 Trace the design. Position the fabric over a pattern and secure the corners with masking tape. Trace the pattern outline directly onto the fabric with a blue-line water erase pen or a pencil.

2 Color the design. Place the fabric on a pad of extra fabric and color areas with regular children's crayons. Color the pattern thoroughly.

3 Iron the piece. Sandwich the fabric between two sheets of plain paper. Iron on the cotton setting to set the crayon colors.

4 Embroider the outline. If desired, back the design with another piece of fabric. Then place the fabric or layers of fabric in an embroidery hoop. Use 3 ply floss to outline the design.

Tea Dye
Dyeing with tea is as easy as 1, 2, 3! Dissolve one heaping tablespoon of instant unsweetened tea per cup of boiling water. Remove the water from heat and soak the fabric in it until the desired shade is achieved. Lay the fabric out flat and allow it to air dry. Press.

PROJECT:
Sunbonnet Sue Quilt

FINISHED SIZE

* 24" wide x 44" long (61 x 112cm)

MATERIALS

* 44" (112cm) wide, 100%
  cotton fabrics:

  * 1¾ yards (1.75m) white for blocks,
    backing, and binding

  * 1¼ yards (1.25m) blue for sashings
    and borders

  * 6" (16cm) squares of 7
    complementary blue fabrics
    for appliqués

* 28" x 50" (71.1 x 127cm) piece of batting

* 3 skeins of DMC 6 ply embroidery
  floss to match the darkest blue fabric

* White sewing thread

* Size 8 embroidery needle

* Sharp no. 2 pencil

* Small embroidery hoop (optional)

* Freezer paper

CUTTING

* Cut 8 white 9" (23cm) squares.

* Cut 1 white 28" x 40" (71.1 x 101.6cm)
  piece for backing.

* Cut 4 white 1¼" x 42" (3.2 x 106.7cm)
  strips (sew them together end to
  end) for the binding.

* Cut 4 blue 2½" x 8½" (6.4 x 21.6cm)
  strips for sashings.

* Cut 3 blue 2½" x 18½" (6.4 x 47cm)
  strips for sashings.

* Cut 2 blue 3½" x 24½" (8.9 x 62.3cm)
  strips for the top and bottom borders.

* Cut 2 blue 3½" x 44" (8.9 x 111.8cm)
  strips for the side borders.

* Cut 8 freezer paper
  9" (23cm) squares.

Sunbonnet Sue is a traditional quilt motif.
Here, she's doing her daily chores. Use the
quilt to teach a child how to read the days of
the week—and to help with household tasks!

Pattern on pages 98–99. Photocopy at 200%.

INSTRUCTIONS

1 Follow the instructions on page 15 to back each 9" (23cm) white square with freezer paper and transfer the embroidery designs. Embroider the squares. Trace the outline of the shaded areas of the pattern onto the right side of the blue squares. Use a different shade of blue fabric for the bonnet and skirt of each girl. Add a ³⁄₁₆" (0.5cm) seam allowance around all edges. Cut out the appliqué pieces, turn the edges under ³⁄₁₆" (0.5cm), and sew each in place. Press the squares. Trim the squares to 8½" x 8½" (21.6 x 21.6cm), making sure the design is centered.

2 Use a ¼" (0.6cm) seam allowance throughout. With right sides facing, sew an embroidered block on either side of a blue 8½" (21.6cm) sashing strip to make 4 block rows. Press the seams toward the blue strips.

3 With right sides facing, sew block rows alternately with 24½" (62.3cm) blue sashing strips to assemble the quilt top as shown in the illustration. Press the seams toward the sashings.

4 Mark each blue top, bottom, and side border strip 3" (7.6cm) from each end. With right sides facing, center and sew the top and bottom border strips in place, aligning the marks with the outer edges of the quilt. Press the seams toward the borders.

5 Sew the side borders in place in the same manner as the top and bottom borders. Miter each corner of the borders. Press the seams toward the borders.

6 Layer the white backing, batting, and assembled top to form a sandwich. Baste all the layers together.

7 Quilt as desired.

8 Remove the basting stitches. Trim the backing and batting even with the top.

9 Bind the edges with the white 1¼" (3.2cm) strips.

Quilt Assembly Diagram

PROJECT:
Lady's Pets Potholders

FINISHED SIZE

* 20" wide x 14" long (50 x 35cm) for entire piece with potholders attached

MATERIALS

* 1½ yards (1.5m) muslin for hanger and potholders (front and back)

* 1½ yards (1.5m) bonded cotton batting for hanger and potholders

* Chipboard for hanger

* Bonded cotton quilt batting or denim for filling

* Double-fold bias binding/tape

* Size 8 embroidery needle

* Sewing threads and needles

* Crayons and an iron

Decorative potholders were popular in the 1930s and 40s, and tinting was frequently used on them. Sets often included two or three hotpads and some kind of hanging pocket or rack for storage. Hang this coordinated set in any kitchen to add a charming vignette!

Pattern on page 213. Photocopy at 200%.

INSTRUCTIONS

1 For the circular potholders, cut six 10" (25.5cm) squares of muslin cloth, two for each potholder. Transfer a design to the center of each square. Add crayon tinting to the design. Embroider the designs.

2 Center and cut each embroidered piece along the circle outline. Cut a muslin back piece. For each potholder, cut two pieces of bonded cotton quilt batting. Sandwich the batting between the front and back pieces. To finish the edges, wrap the edge with double fold bias tape. Stitch in place by hand.

3 For the half circle potholder hanger, cut two 20" x 10" (51 x 25.5cm) pieces of muslin for the front and back. Transfer the design to the center of the front fabric. Add crayon tinting to the design. Embroider the design.

4 Cut a crescent-shaped piece of chipboard the same shape as the pattern outline to fit the hanger piece. Cut two pieces of bonded cotton quilt batting as padding for the hanger.

5 Center the embroidered piece over the chipboard and cut the fabric ½" (1.5cm) larger than the board on all sides. Use the trimmed fabric piece as a pattern to cut another piece of muslin for the back.

6 Fold the seam allowance on the back piece up over the crescent board. Fold back the seam allowance on the embroidered front and whip stitch the pieces of fabric together around all edges. Finish the edge with double fold bias binding. Attach a loop to the top center of the hanger using bias binding.

PROJECT:
Tea Time Quilt

FINISHED SIZE

* 18½" wide x 43" long (47 x 109cm)

MATERIALS

* 44" (112cm) wide, 100% cotton fabrics:
  * ½ yard (0.5m) bleached muslin fabric for design blocks
  * ⅛ yard (0.2m) wide-striped fabric for word strips
  * ⅛ yard (0.2m) dark blue fabric for inner borders
  * ⅜ yard (0.4m) light blue print fabric for outer borders
  * ¾ yard (0.75m) of fabric for backing and binding
* 24" x 48" (61 x 122cm) piece of quilt batting
* Skeins of assorted embroidery flosses
* Blue and white sewing threads

CUTTING

* Cut 4 white 5¾" x 12" (14.6 x 30.5cm) pieces for design blocks.
* Cut 5 striped 3½" x 12" (8.9 x 30.5cm) pieces for word blocks.
* Cut 2 dark blue 1½" x 12" (3.8 x 30.5cm) strips for the inner borders (for the top and bottom).
* Cut 2 dark blue 1½" x 40" (3.8 x 101.6cm) strips for the inner borders (for the sides).
* Cut 2 light blue 2½" x 13½" (6.4 x 34.3cm) strips for the outer borders (for the top and bottom).
* Cut 2 light blue 2½" x 44" (6.4 x 111.8cm) strips for the outer borders (for the sides).
* Cut 1 light blue 24" x 48" (61 x 121.9cm) piece for the backing.
* Cut 4 light blue 1½" x 42" (3.8 x 106.7cm) strips (sew them together end to end) for the binding.

Stitch and piece this darling quilt and its clever saying for your favorite room... or favorite lady!

Pattern on page 122. Photocopy at 200%.

INSTRUCTIONS

Note: Use ¼" (0.6cm) seam allowances throughout.

1 To make the design blocks, transfer the designs to the center of the design and word blocks, referring to the photo. Embroider the designs and words. Press each design.

2 With right sides facing, sew the first word block above the top design block. Sew alternating word and design blocks to the bottom of the first one, following the sequence shown in the photo.

3 With right sides facing, sew the dark blue top and bottom inner border strips in place. Trim the ends even. Press the seams toward the border strips.

4 With right sides facing, sew the dark blue side inner border strips in place. Trim the ends even. Press the seams toward the border strips.

5 With right sides facing, sew the light blue top and bottom border strips in place. Trim the ends even. Press the seams toward the border strips.

6 With right sides facing, sew the light blue side border strips in place. Trim the ends even. Press the seams toward the border strips.

7 Layer the backing, batting, and the assembled top to form a sandwich. Center the top on the batting. Baste the layers together.

8 Quilt the piece as desired.

9 Remove the basting stitches. Trim the backing and batting even with the edges of the quilt top.

10 Bind the edges with the light blue 1½" (3.8cm) strips. With right sides facing, sew the strip ends together. Press the seams open. Sew the strips to the back of the quilt and fold back ¼" (0.6cm) along raw edge. Fold over and whip stitch in place.

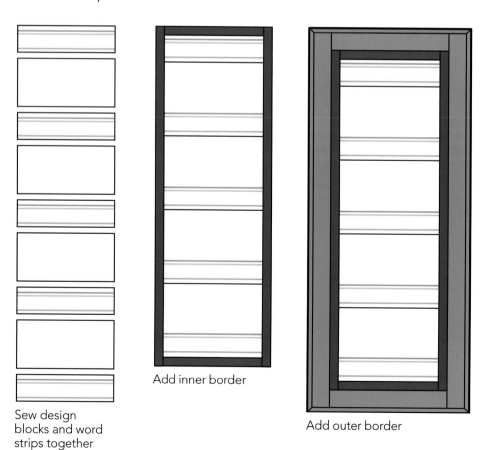

Sew design
blocks and word
strips together

Add inner border

Add outer border

PROJECT:
Doggie Laundry Bag

FINISHED SIZE

* 16" wide x 23" long (41 x 59cm)

MATERIALS

* 1 yard (1m) white fabric
* ⅔ yard (0.7m) print fabric
* Embroidery floss
* Embroidery needle
* 4 yards (4m) bias tape
* Crayons

CUTTING

* Cut 2 white rectangles 16" x 23" (41 x 59cm). Round the corners.
* Cut 1 print rectangles 8½" x 16" (22 x 41cm). Round the corners.

Laundry bags like these aren't as popular anymore, but they should be! This bag is almost too precious for dirty socks. You can use it for wash supplies and clothespins instead! The combination of a vintage reproduction fabric with this cute dog pattern is just perfect.

Pattern on page 32. Photocopy at 200%.

INSTRUCTIONS

1 Cut a 9½" (24cm) slit in the front of bag, following the image.

2 Finish the slit edges with bias tape.

3 Curve the print rectangle on the bottom to match the bag. Curve the top as shown in photo.

4 Finish the top edge of the pocket with bias tape.

5 Fold the pocket in the middle. Press. Line up the pocket with the bottom of the bag. Sew the pocket to the bag along the fold, creating two sections of pocket.

6 Trace the embroidery pattern onto the front of the bag.

7 Color tint as desired. See instructions for tinting with crayons on page 17.

8 Embroider the design.

9 Layer the front and back of the bag with wrong sides facing so the edges line up.

10 Finish the edges with bias tape.

Patterns

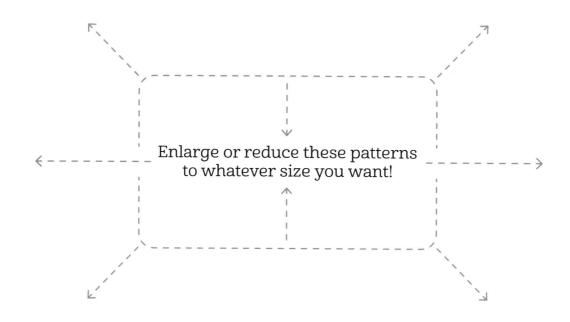

Enlarge or reduce these patterns to whatever size you want!

Row of Wreaths

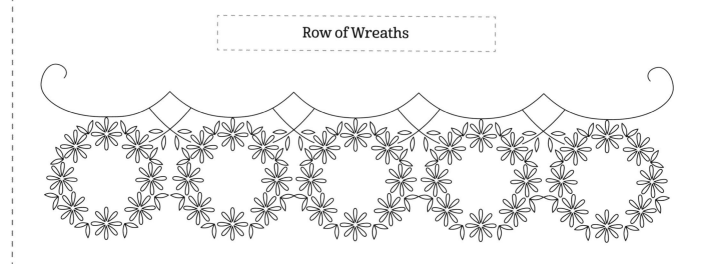

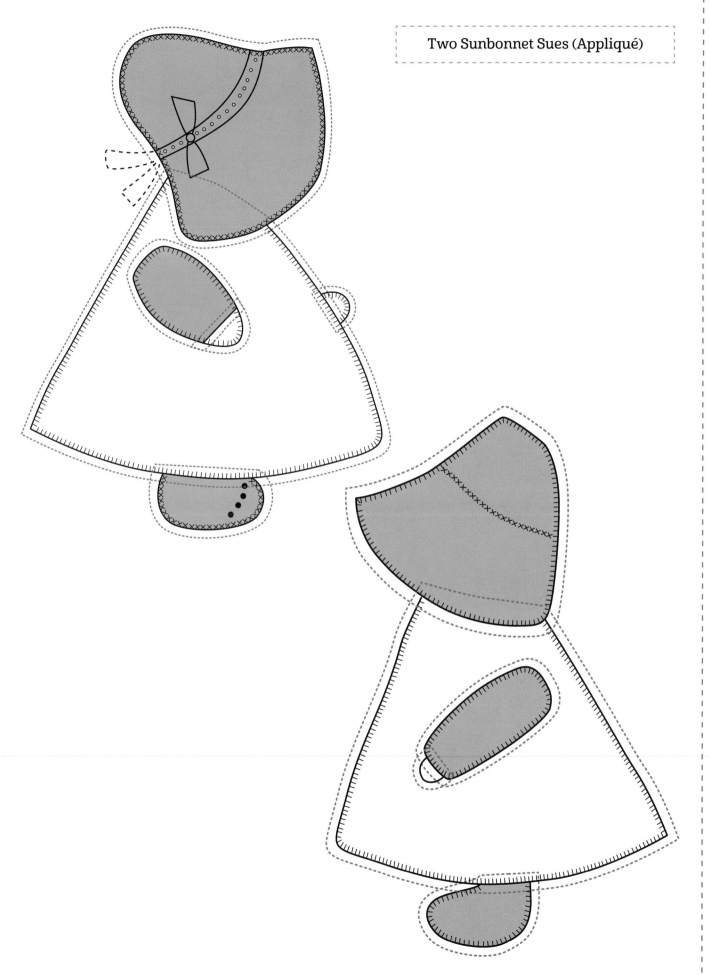

Two Sunbonnet Sues (Appliqué)

Sunday

Monday

Tuesday

Wednesday

Thursday

Friday

Saturday

Good Morning and Good Night Set

Rose Vine

Curious Puppy

Animal Trio Set (Appliqué)

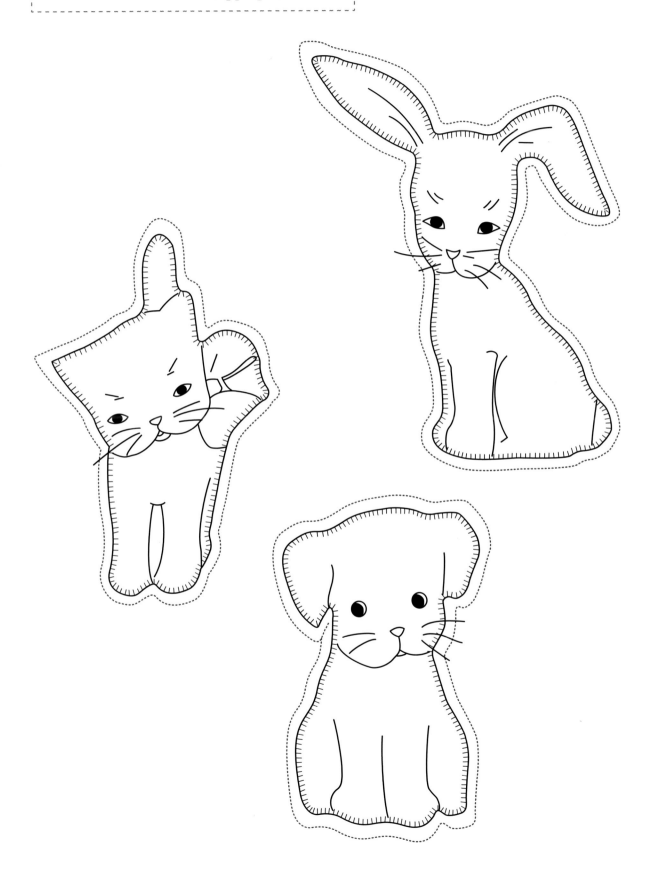

Doggie Laundry Bag

Rooster and Hen

Modern Women Set

Kitty Romance

Hammock Kittens

Helping with Laundry

Lovely Laundry Lady

Perfect Portrait

Basket and Ribbon

Heart and Roses

"His" Flower Basket

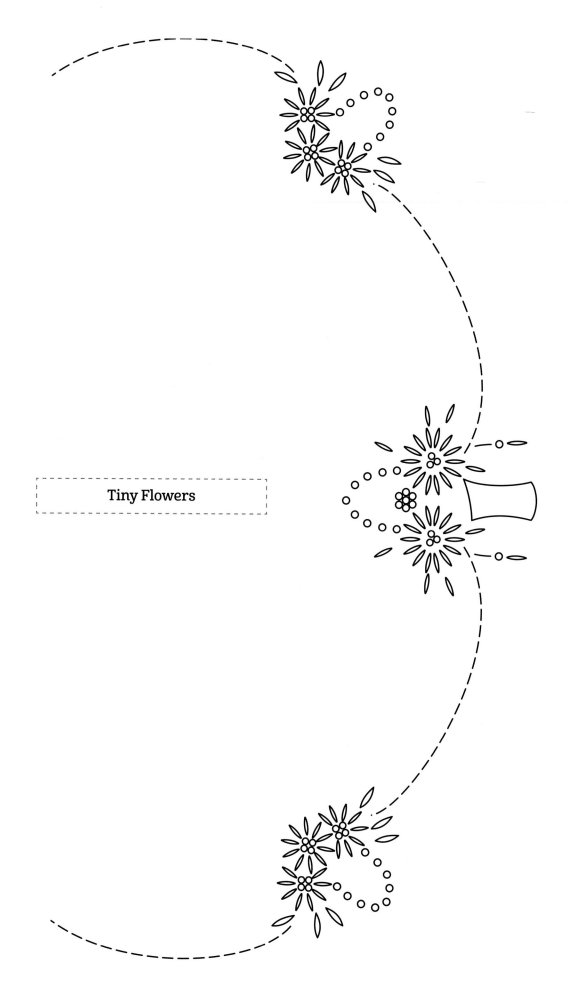

Tiny Flowers

Vase Bouquet

Sharing Secrets

Lady with Parasol

Lady with Flowers

Pair of Birds

Days of the Week Kittens

SUNDAY

WEDNESDAY

THURSDAY

MONDAY

TUESDAY

FRIDAY

SATURDAY

Bird Bearing Flowers

Bird in a Basket

Shoes Set

Fruit Basket

Bow Wow Wickets

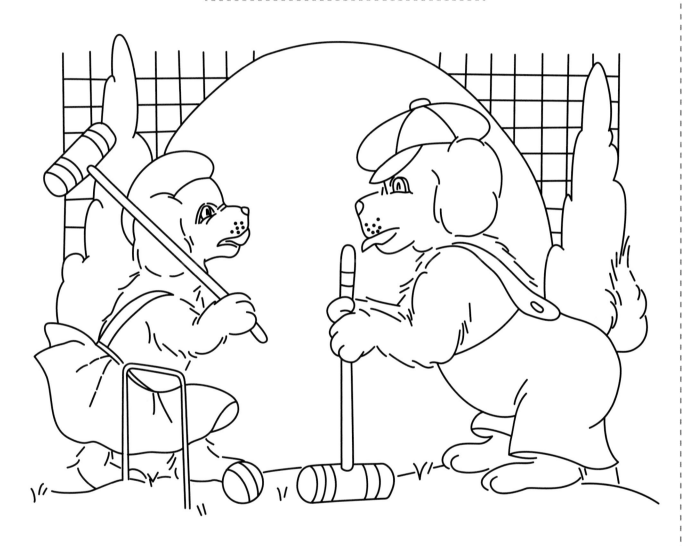

Horse and Carriage

Flower Wreath

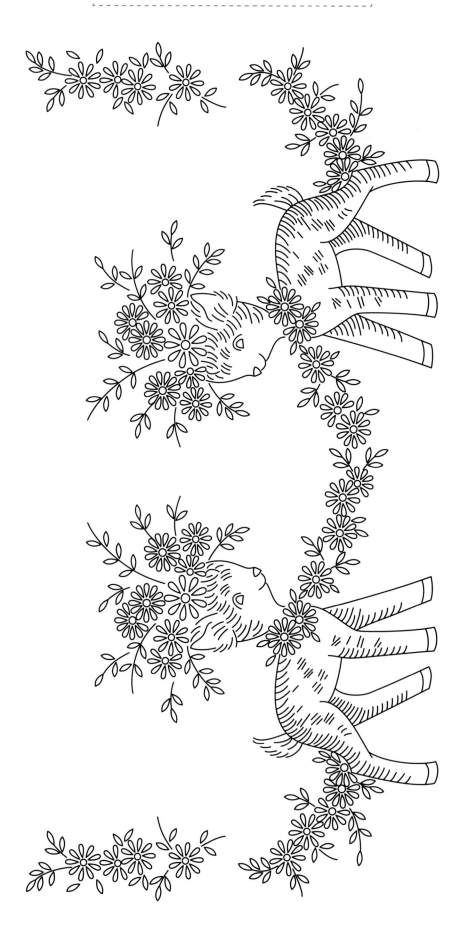

Darling Deer

Good Luck Horseshoe

Flowers and Bows

Nest Builders

Chef and Fruit Set

Pink Ruffles Nosegay

Waiting

A Butterfly Visit

Pretty Profile

Turtle and Terriers

Cupid

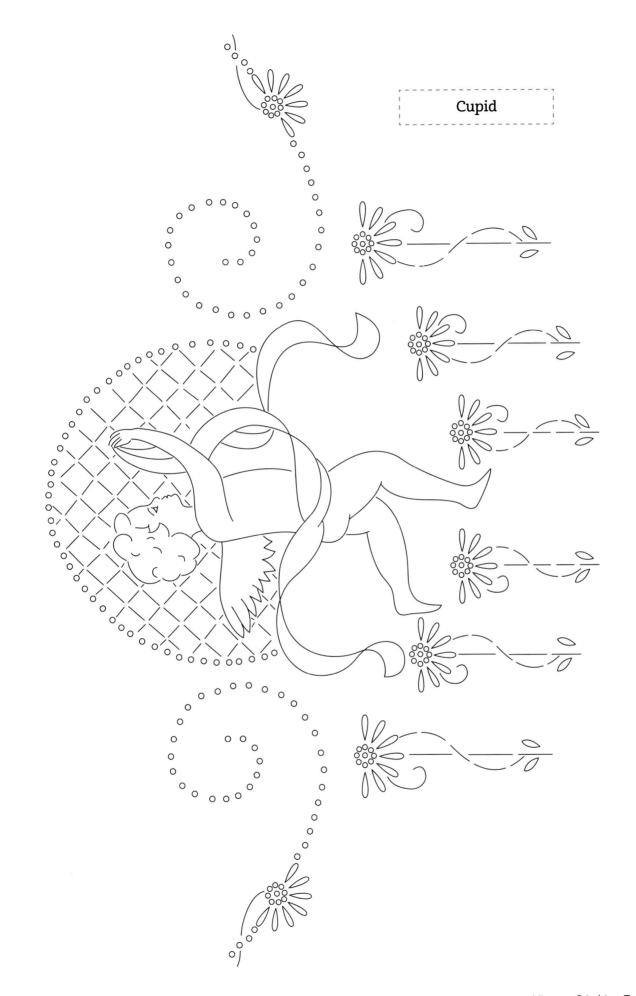

Spiky Flowers

Musical Puppies

Puppy with Pipe

Hat Ladies Set

Dogs with Butterflies

Bowser's Big Band

Close Friends

Double and Single Flower Set

Bountiful Basket

Big Flower

Bird and Clothespin

Basic Alphabet

ABCDEFGHIJ
KLMNOPQRS
TUVWXYZ

abcdefghijklmn
opqrstuvwxyz

Girl at the Gate

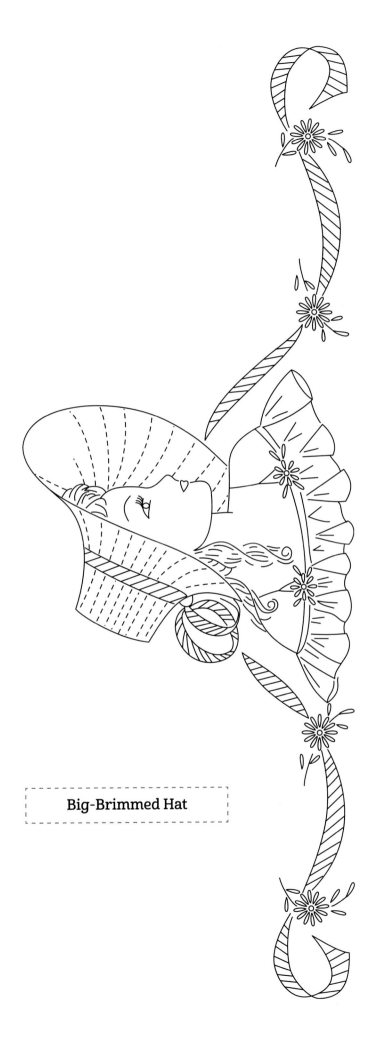

Big-Brimmed Hat

Twin Sisters Set

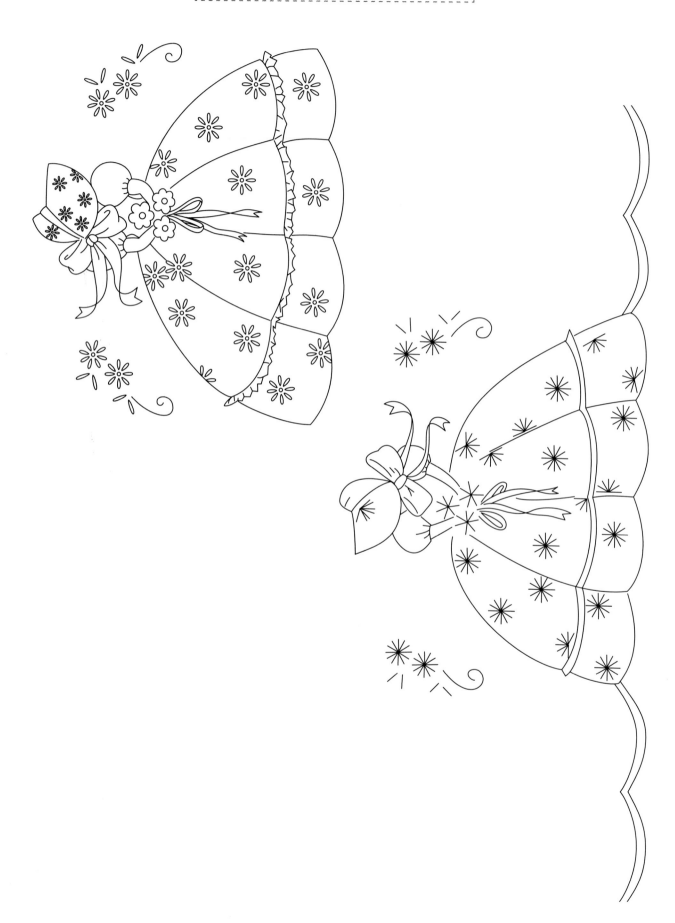

Puppy Love

Basket Kittens

Flying Bird

Singing Bird

Little Animals Set (Appliqué)

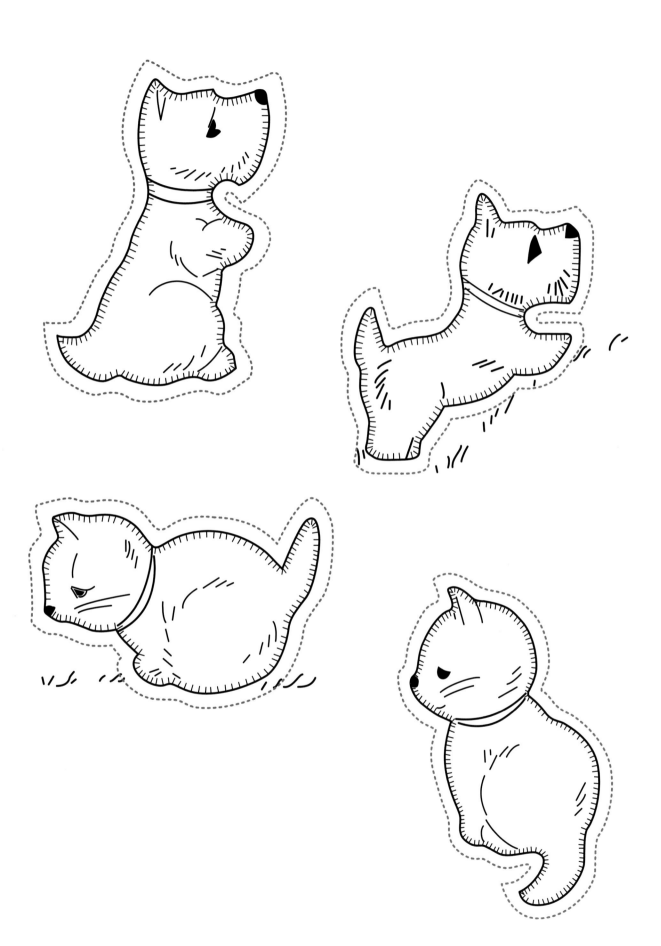

Purses Set

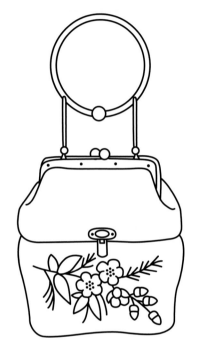

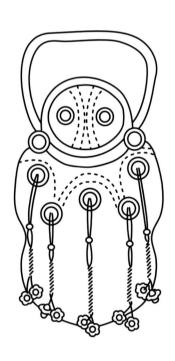

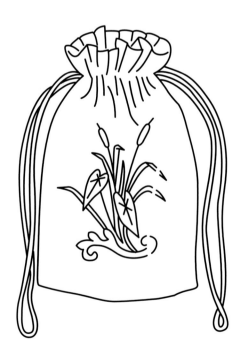

Circus Elephant

Forest Fawn

Puppy Cowboy

Peeking Pups

Homekeeping Hearts are Happiest.

SUNDAY — CHURCH

MONDAY — WASH

TUESDAY — IRON

WEDNESDAY — MEND

THURSDAY — MARKET

FRIDAY — CLEAN

SATURDAY — GARDEN

Bears at Play

Spray Bouquet

Flowery Parasol

Fan with Ribbon

Four Lady's Days Set

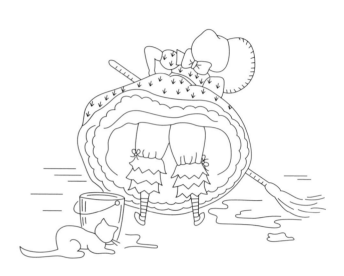

Dancing Duck

Basket Puppies

Fancy Lady Faces Set

Hidden Kitty

Flowered Heart

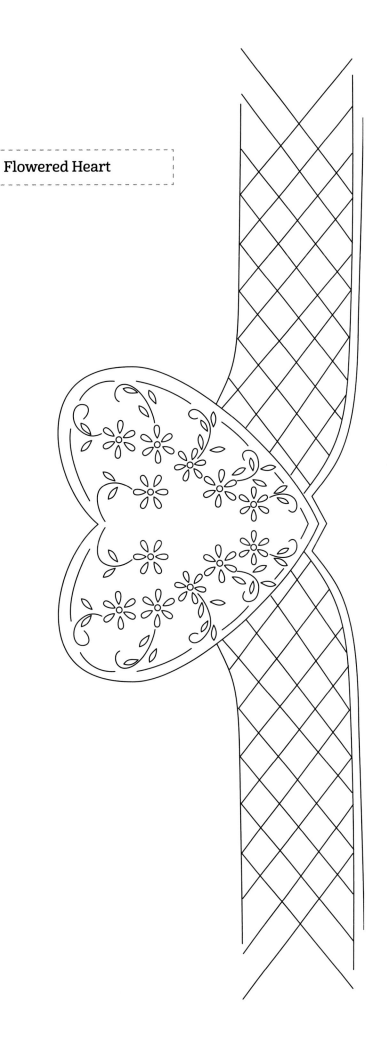

Baby Animals Set

Butterfly Border

Sampler Flower Bouquet

Daily Chores Set

CHURCH
ON-SUNDAY

WASH
ON-MONDAY

VISIT
ON-THURSDAY

IRON
ON-TUESDAY

SEW
ON-WEDNESDAY

CLEAN
ON-FRIDAY

BAKE
ON-SATURDAY

Blossom Scape

Belle Bouquet

Busy Bears Set

Eating Birds

Funny Puppy

Tea Time Quilt Set

A Woman is Like a Tea-Bag...You Never Know How Strong She is Until She Gets in Hot Water.

Women's Work

A Man Works from Sun to Sun,

Woman's Work is Never Done.

Lady in a Bowl

Serving Cake

Bonnet Babe with Laundry

Dotty Border

Three Flowers

Days of the Week Drop Capitals

Monday

Tuesday

Wednesday

Thursday

Friday

Saturday

Sunday

Fiddler Dog

Three Little Pigs

Bunnies on a Bicycle

Flowery Boot

Teapots Set

Pitcher and Bowl

Donkey and Cart

Bowl of Lilacs

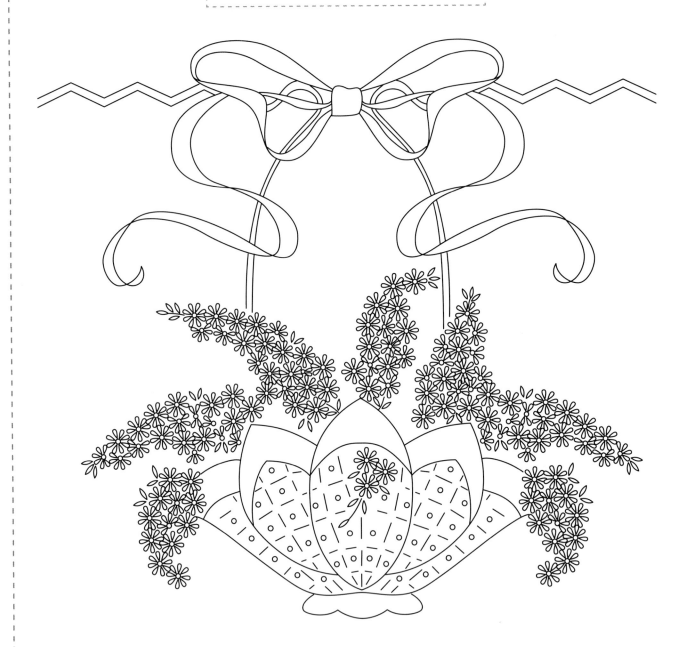

Two Flowers in a Basket

Cute Animals Set

Little House (Appliqué)

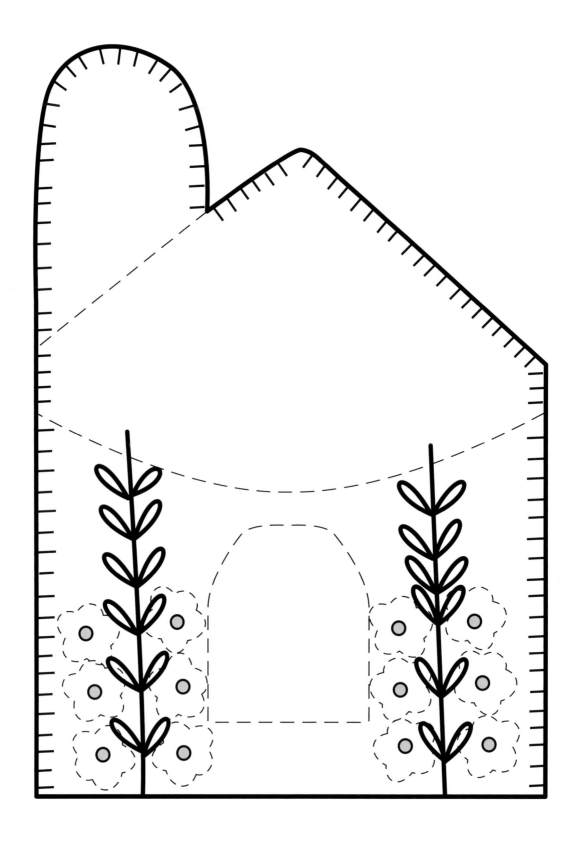

Lady in Apron

Three Blossoms

Morning Glories

Double Trouble

Overflowing Bouquet

Basket of Little Flowers

Tall Flower Basket

Big Bows and Little Flowers

A Lady's Home

Days of the Week Outline

MONDAY

TUESDAY

WEDNESDAY

THURSDAY

FRIDAY

SATURDAY

SUNDAY

Listening to the Radio

Goose Girl

Just Playing

Pansies in a Fan Basket

Flowery Mailbox

Organized Lady's Week Set

WEDNESDAY

THURSDAY

FRIDAY

SATURDAY

Silverware Girl

Sailor Boy

Clown Puppy (Appliqué)

Puppies in Cups Set

Beribboned Basket

Basket of Lilacs

Cornucopias

Magnolias

Busy Children Set

Seesaw Fun

Scottie Potholder Set

POTS-PANS

Windy Washing

Picking Flowers

Chef and Dasterdly Dog

Waitress and Chef Set

Rose Bouquet

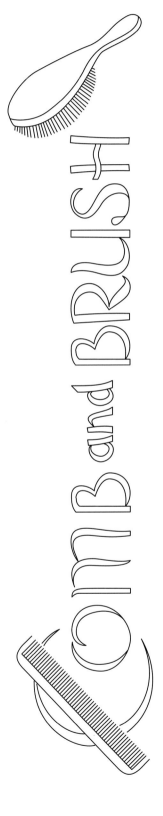

Comb and Brush

Comb and Brush Set

Elegant Ladies Set

Three Teddy Bears

Cat and Dog

Grapes

Fun for Two

Bunny Go Round

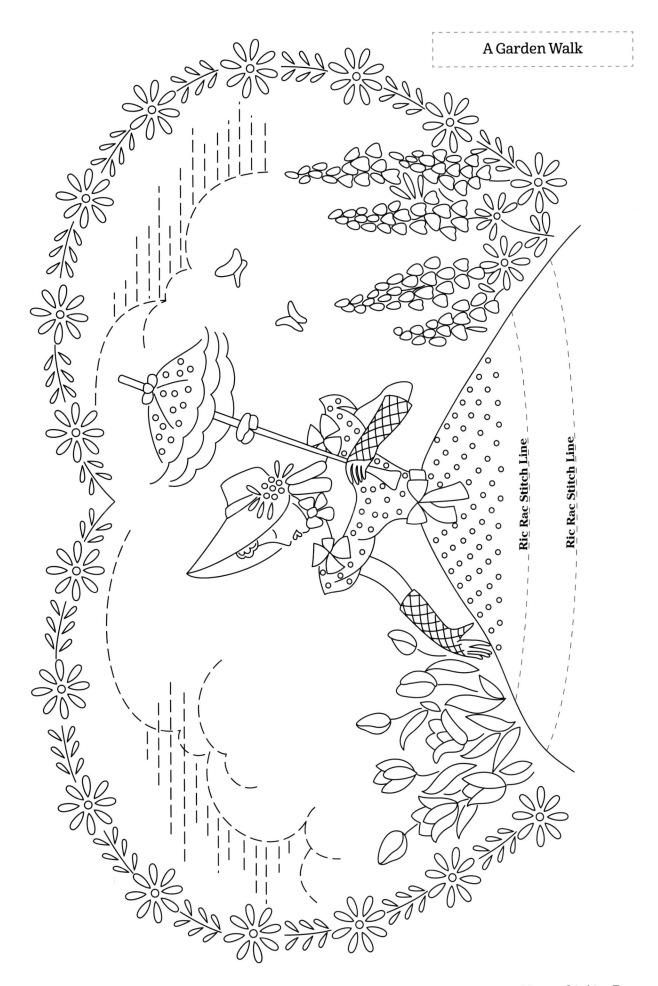

A Garden Walk

Ric Rac Stitch Line

Ric Rac Stitch Line

Flowered Skirt

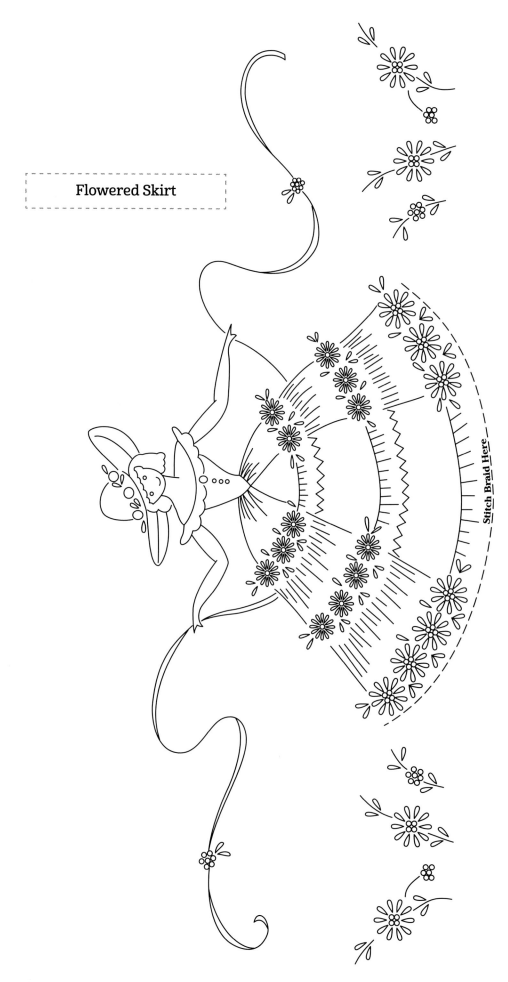

Stitch Braid Here

Days of the Week

SUNDAY
MONDAY
TUESDAY
WEDNESDAY
THURSDAY
FRIDAY
SATURDAY

Animal Set

Acorns and Oak Leaves

Bunny Ride

Seesaw Friends

Basket of Strawberries

Star Flowers

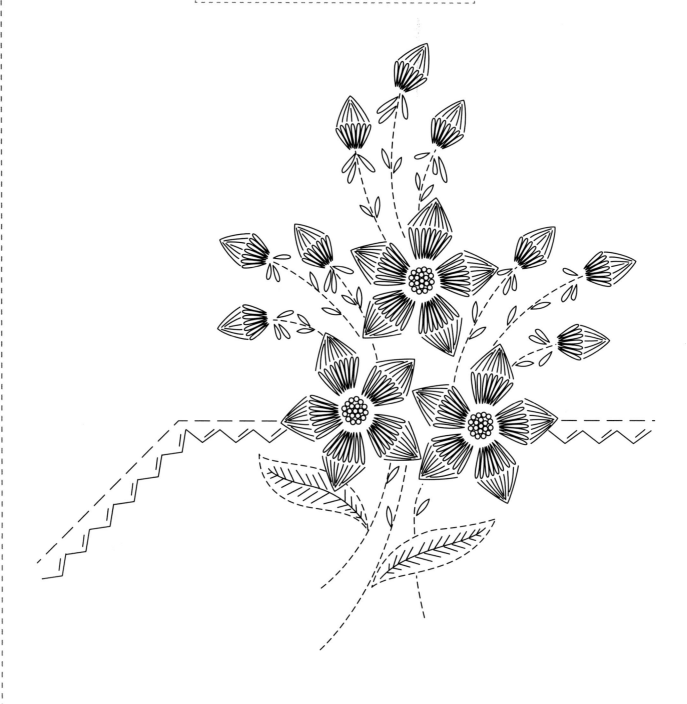

Fun Farm Friends Set

Dancing Ladies

Dreams of Leisure

Scotties Rhyme Set

morning

evening

it's eat

and frolic

jump

be happy

Daisies in a Bow

Two Big Flowers

Butterflies and Basket

Time to Play

Modern Misses Set

Scalloped Wreath

Basket of Daisies

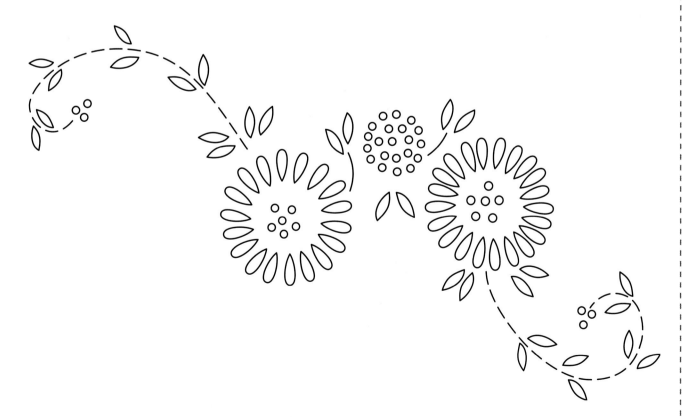

Help in the Kitchen

Lady's Pets Potholders Set

POTS

Kitten and Scottie Dog

Puppies with Heart

Laundry on a Windy Day

Basket of Poppies

Framed Lady

Sheerly Sensational

Profile of a Lady

Women and Men

Women like ~ the simpler things in life – (MEN)!

Men like ~ the important things in life – (WOMEN)!

Days of the Week Best Friends Set

MARKET ON THURSDAY

BAKE ON FRIDAY

CLEAN ON SATURDAY

CHURCH ON SUNDAY

Sassy Kitty